Here's what
Jannah Je

I can't continue withou
Muslim Girls! No damsels in distress, no dominating male protagonist,
no cliché girly nonsense! ... This is exactly what our girls need to grow
up reading.
–Emma Apple, Author of best-selling 'Children's First Questions'
Islamic Book Series

The Jannah Jewels books are awesome. They have made my daughters
love to read with characters that dress like them and names they are
familiar with. The stories keep their attention and make them curious
about times past and present. We love Jannah Jewels at our house.
-Jessica Colon

The Jannah Jewels series are exactly what I would write if I had the
gift of creative writing! As a mother, they are fun to read aloud as
well as for the child to get immersed in! This series is the perfect blend
of history, mystery, adventure and Islam! My daughter has even
recommended these to her non-Muslim friends and was inspired
to do a 'show and tell' on Mansa Musa thanks to these books! I'm
thankful for these engaging stories and the strong female characters,
thank you to the authors for a job well done, we can't wait for the rest
of the series!
-Nazia Ullah

I like how you combine adventure and Islamic concepts to make us
readers want to know more and more about the series. I am addicted
to Jannah Jewels and I can't wait to find when and how they will get
the artifact in America!
-Subhana Saad, Age 8

Fantastic book! My child was turning pages and couldn't wait to read
the next chapter. So much so he's asking for the next book in the series.
-Mrs. S. A. Khanom, Book Reviewer

Our 8 year old had lost interest in reading and Jannah Jewels got her back to it. Not only that, this series has been our favourite gift to our children's friends and cousins and we hear children have a tendency to get hooked to these books!
-Umm Fatima

I have been reading Jannah Jewels for a long time and I love all the characters in this series. I can see myself in Hidayah and Iman, and I feel as if I'm in the actual story! I hope you love these books as much as I do!
-Fiza Ali, Age 10

I just wanted to thank you for these amazing books! I have 3 daughters, two of which are school age and they have recently been reading lots of Ninja Go books. We've been trying to find a better alternative for them to read and stumbled upon these, they are just wonderful! My girls are excited to read them, find them action filled and fun, while we don't need to worry about excessive violence or inappropriate language in the content. My life feels easier now thanks to these books, thank you SO much for your contribution to the Ummah, loving this series and we're looking forward to many books to come!
-Suzanne C.

My 8 year old has enjoyed these books immensely, she managed to finish each book in 2 days and has asked for more! We have made a small book club amongst our friends to swap and share the books, as mothers we love the strong role models the characters provide. We are looking forward to more books in the series!
-Falak Pasha

A captivating series with a rhythmic quest. Some of the books in the series also have surprises that made me jump into the next book right away. It's hard to put down, but at the same time I don't want to finish the book I'm reading unless there's another one waiting for me.
-Misbah Rabbani

We loved the Jannah Jewels books! There are very few Muslim books for kids that are entertaining. The Jannah Jewels books were very fun to read. They were so good that we read the entire series in two days!
-Zayd & Sofia Tayeb, age 10 & 7

"I like reading books in a series, but the Jannah Jewels is especially great because I can look forward to a whole new place in history with every book. I also love the different personalities of the heroines, and my favourite is Iman because I love animals and riding horses too."
-Sarah Gamar, age 10

I have a 9 year old boy and 5 year old girl. Both are very good readers now only because of Jannah Jewels. There are times when they were addicted to the screen. But Jannah Jewels changed everything upside down. The interesting characters, way of narration, adventure, artwork and messages make it more real in my kids' world and help them take the morals to heart. It changed their behavior a lot and made them good kids.
-Shaniya Arafath

My 8 year old loves this series - so much so that she has told all her friends about it, and one of them even gifted a couple more Jannah Jewels books for her birthday! In fact, I found myself reading her books much to the delight of my daughter - and then we both discussed our favorite parts. I love how the writers combine Islamic history with fun story lines and cute picture depictions. My daughter loves to sketch - and her books are filled with the Jannah Jewels character drawings. I would buy this series again and again. Thank you for all your wonderful work!
-Ruku Kazia

Learning about Islamic history and famous Muslims of the past makes these books a historical book lover's wish, and the Islamic twist is a plus for young Muslim readers. Jannah Jewels has been Muslimommy approved as kid-friendly!
-Zakiyya Osman, MusliMommy.com

I love all of the Jannah Jewels books, and the fact that you combine history and adventure in your stories. I also liked that you put the holy verses of Quran that remind us to stay close to Allah and I liked the fact that in one book you mentioned the verse from Quran which mentions the benefit of being kind to your enemy. I have read all of the Jannah Jewels books and even read two of these books in one day, that's how much I like these books!
–Fatima Bint Saifurrehman, Age 8

My kids liked the characters because they are modest in their mannerisms and dress, so that was something my daughter could relate to. Even though the characters are girls, it had enough excitement and the presence of supporting male characters to be read by both girls and boys. Throughout the book there was an essence of Islamic values and there was a lot of adventure to keep us guessing!
-HomeStudyMama, Book Reviewer

"We just can't thank you enough, Alhamdulillah! I just recently noticed all the characters in each book are actually real! MashaAllah, what a wonderful way to introduce them to Islamic history. I home educate my children and we are hoping to use each book as a syllabus for our world history now. Allah reward you for creating such an inspiration for our young today!"
-Umm Aasiyah

It's important for girls and boys, Muslim and not, to have strong, non-stereotyped female role models. Jannah jewels bring that in a unique way with a twist on time travel, fantasy, super heroes and factual Muslim history. It is beautifully written, engaging and an absolute must for any Muslim (and non-Muslim) kids library! My daughter LOVES The Jannah Jewels...
–Hani, Book Reviewer

We've reviewed 100s of Islamic non-fiction and fiction books from every single continent, except Antarctica, and none of the fiction books have made such an impression on our family as Jannah Jewels.
–Ponn M. Sabra, Best-selling author, AmericanMuslimMom.com

By Umm Nura

Vancouver

*To Inaya who lovingly reminds us that we are blessed to be in His
Divine Care – U.N.*

Published by Gentle Breeze Books, Vancouver, B.C., Canada

Copyright 2017 by Umm Nura
Illustrations by Clarice Menguito

Visit us on the Web! www.JannahJewels.com

ISBN: 978-1-988337-04-3

June 2017

Contents

Prologue 1

Weight on their Shoulders 5

Focus and Faith..12

Sands of the Past 23

Hidden Pharaohs...33

Muezza 43

Jumpy Cat 53

A Very Super Market..65

Friend or Foe 73

Desperate Enemies...85

The Glass Lamp 92

The History of History 102

Reunited 112

Glossary 120

Sport:

Archery

Role:

Guides and leads the girls

Superpower:

Intense sight and spiritual insight

Fear:

Spiders

Special Gadget:

Ancient Compass

Carries:

Bow and Arrow, Ancient Map, Compass

HIDAYAH

JAIDE

Sport:

Skateboarding

Role:

Artist, Racer

Superpower:

Fast racer on foot or skateboard

Fear:

Hunger (She's always hungry!)

Special Gadget:

Time Travel Watch

Carries:

Skateboard, Sketchpad, Pencil, Watch

Sport:

Horseback Riding

Role:

Walking Encyclopedia,
Horseback Rider

Superpower:

Communicates with
animals

Fear:

Heights

Special Gadget:

Book of Knowledge

Carries:

Book of Knowledge, has
horse named "Spirit"

IMAN

SARA

Sport:

Swimming

Role:

Environmentalist,
Swimmer

Superpower:

Breathes underwater for
a long time

Fear:

Drowning

Special Gadget:

Metal Ball

Carries:

Sunscreen, Water
canteen, Metal Ball

SUPPORTING CHARACTERS

JAFFAR

JASMIN

MOE

SLIM

THE JANNAH JEWELS ADVENTURE 11

EGYPT

ARTIFACT 8: MAMLUK ENAMELLED LAMP

"Use your own guidance, such as the lessons you have learned from your Master and each other, and let that direct you. Allah will protect you and guide you."

~ Master Swimmer to the Jannah Jewels

As salaamu alaikum Dear Readers,

We are just two artifacts away from finding out the secret in the Golden Clock! What could it be?

In the last book, Intrigue in India, we learned that someone tried to rig the big talent show and tried to foil Hidayah's talents. Instead Hidayah persevered and we all learned valuable lessons in the importance of diversity.

In this book, the Jannah Jewels travel back into time to Egypt and meet a very curious cat, visit the great Al Azhar University and meet ibn Khaldun, the famous historian.

Come along, dear reader, and immerse yourself into the wonders of Egypt. The Jannah Jewels must work quickly if they want to make it to the great Archery Battle. Let's go on this adventure!

With warmest salaams,
Umm Nura

Prologue

Long ago, in the ancient Moroccan walled city of Fes, a decision was made. The great and peaceful Master Archer had reached old age and had to choose an apprentice to take his place and be trusted with the enormous task of protecting the world from the forces of evil. As Master Archer, he carried a deep Secret — one that no one else knew. To keep it hidden, the Secret was written upon a scroll, placed into a box and locked away in a giant Golden Clock. Who would keep this Golden Clock safe from the hands of evil after him? This decision would affect the future and balance of the world and had to be made with care and clarity.

He watched his students of archery very carefully, many of whom wanted to be chosen by their Master. Two of his students stood out to him like no other: Layla and Khan. Layla was flawless in her aim and light on her feet, who knew how to focus hard with her vision and her heart. She wanted nothing more than to bring peace into the world and use her skills in that way. Khan, on the other hand, was a fierce-fighter with strong hands and swift strategies and worked extra hard to gain his Master's attention. He had been practicing archery since he was old enough to hold a bow and learned the art from his older brother Idrees—a highly-trained senior student of the Master's.

The day finally came for the Master Archer to choose his successor and become the next Guardian of the Golden Clock and its Secret. Who would take on this great responsibility?

To everyone's surprise, he chose a woman to be the next Master Archer, the first time in history. Layla humbly accepted and continued to train relentlessly to prepare for this new role.

"Only those who are peaceful and know how to control their anger may possess the secrets of the Bow and Arrow," the Master Archer told all his students. "You must carry great humility and selflessness to lead others. Only then will you be followed."

Many of the Master's students respected and honored his decision, including Khan. He admired

Layla for her nobility and knew she must deserve this honor if the Master had chosen her over him and all the other students. Soon thereafter, he sent for her hand in marriage, and her family accepted.

The majority of the village rejoiced at their blessed union except for a few of the original Master's students. After the Master Archer announced his decision, this group of angry and disappointed students banded together and decided to leave the institution. Over time their anger turned into greed and jealousy. They spread rumors about Khan saying that he only married Layla to gain power and get his hands on the Golden Clock. They devised plans to separate the two great archers and steal the Clock along with its great Secret.

Layla and Khan were unaware of these terrible schemes. Khan went on to become a successful businessman and a leader of his community. The couple lived happily practicing the ways of the Bow and Arrow together whenever time permitted. They were blessed with two children: a boy named Jaffar and a girl named Jasmin. Jaffar was a gentle and curious spirit who loved to practice calligraphy and read as many books as he could. Jasmin was quite the opposite as she loved to play all kinds of sports, tumble and practice archery like her mother.

Khan had great expectations of his son and would push him to practice archery more. Jaffar was not a natural at it like Jasmin, nor had as much interest in it as her. To please his father, he would practice every day with Jasmin, although he just wanted to read and write. Jasmin enjoyed teaching her brother and loved being praised by her father. The family lived peacefully in their villa for some time until the day came that everything changed…

1

Weight on their Shoulders

"But… who tried to poison you in India?" Sensei Elle questioned in a worried tone.

The girls looked at each other, thinking back through everything that had happened.

"I don't…" Hidayah trailed off.

Jasmin finished her thought, "...we don't know!" But in the back of Jasmin's mind, suspicions formed into ideas. She suspected that her brother, Jaffar, might still be working against them. Or perhaps Moe and Slim were still working for someone. Whoever it was, he got very close to poisoning Hidayah, and who knew what the next plan could be.

"Ladies, I know it is frightening to be so close to

enemies trying to harm you," Sensei Elle, the Master Archer, reassured the Jannah Jewels. "When I had to leave my family to flee attackers and protect the secret of the clock, I was very afraid. But I was able to focus on my faith in Allah to get me through."

"I once had to harvest pearls to help Sensei Elle repair the broken crown of a Bahrani Queen," the Master Swimmer explained. "I almost drowned trying to find the right oysters."

The Master Artist stepped in, "and I was once tricked by a mad inventor who made me draw diagrams of his mad ideas. I had to write code into drawings he was showing Sensei Elle even though I didn't want to.

"That was a great code," Sensei Elle said, smiling and nodding.

"It really was," Master Artist said, satisfied.

"And I once had to ride through a forest fire to retrieve a book vital to our research on mechanics," Master Horse Rider recalled. "My horse was so brave to trust me, and I was so proud of him."

"We tell you these stories to assure you that we

have all faced challenges," Sensei Elle explained. "In many of our missions over the years, we have faced our fears and put ourselves in great danger."

The girls began to realize that they had underestimated how difficult it was to be a Master. They had assumed that mastering their skills was the end of the road. But the Masters spent years protecting secrets, serving those in need, and ensuring the balance of power around time and space.

Jasmin felt worried. She wondered: did she really have what it would take to be the new Master Archer? Was she ready to throw herself into dangerous situations and serve a higher purpose?

But Hidayah felt a calm settle over her. She was not afraid of the responsibilities that becoming Master Archer would lay upon her. She looked forward to being able to lead the Jewels and work with other Masters.

"And," Sensei Elle continued, "we tell you these stories because you are about to embark on the penultimate mission. The clock is falling apart without the last two artifacts, so you must hurry. Your next quest will be very difficult, and you will face trouble several times. Some of you will feel more challenged than others. But you must be brave."

Master Artist added, "Remember, the Qur'an tells us that Allah will increase the guidance of those who are already guided. An excess of good deeds are better in your Lord's sight for reward."

Master Swimmer assured them. "Use your own guidance, such as the lessons you have learned from your Master and each other, and let that direct you. Allah will protect you and guide you."

Master Artist finished, "but to help guide you, we have this clue to help you down the path." She handed Hidayah a slip of paper.

Once you get over the hump, follow your noses. Follow the Prophet's Favorite through the bizarre market to the man who unlocks and illuminates men's minds. He will send you to the key.

"Now go," Sensei Elle whispered. "You have a difficult path ahead of you."

The Jannah Jewels felt exhausted. Jasmin

had questions she wanted to ask her mother. But there was no time to waste. Without even stopping for dinner, the girls turned and pushed themselves into the tree while reciting together, "Bismillah hir Rahman nir Raheem."

*   *   *   *

The air was hot, dry, and stale. The heat was suffocating.

"The desert. We're in the desert," Jaide proclaimed as they landed in the soft, golden sand.

"Oh," Sara chuckled, "you aren't kidding!" She reached down and patted the sand by her feet. As far as the girls could see, there were large, open dunes of golden sand, with no buildings or wildlife. They were sitting on the edge of a small pond, an oasis in the desert, surrounded by a thicket of trees. They might as well have been on an island, though, because there was nothing but sand all around them.

"This is unbelievable! What are we going to do?" Iman said with fear in her voice.

"This is the Sahara," Jasmin said confidently. "I know it."

9

"How do you know?" Hidayah asked. "How can you be so sure?"

Jasmin nodded. "The Sahara stretches all the way out to Morocco. When I was young, my mother and father took me to the dunes of Merzouga, on the edge of the Sahara. It looked just like this. We must be in the dunes of the Sahara."

"Let me look at the map," Hidayah responded, pulling out the map from her bag. "Let's see if there are any artifacts in the Sahara."

The girls unrolled the map across the sand, and sat in a ring around it, each holding a part down against the gentle breeze. As they pointed to each artifact, they retraced their journeys together.

"You know," Sara reflected, "we've really had a grand adventure. I feel like we've learned so much, about history and about ourselves."

They looked at the two remaining artifact markers on the map.

MAMLUK ENAMELLED LAMP

Egypt, North Africa

MAMLUK ORNATE TRUNK

Uzbekistan, Central Asia

"Well, Egypt is one of the two remaining locations, so we really are in the Sahara!" Jaide exclaimed. "But how are we to know when we are?"

2

Focus and Faith

The two hooded figures sat in the tea shop next to the Bou Inania mosque in Fes, watching tourists and vendors walk up and down the busy street. The first pushed his hood back, revealing his face, and raised his glass of sweet tea to his lips.

"Boss is going to be furious, Slim," Moe said, blowing the steam off his glass and taking a small sip of the drink. "He told us to stop the Jannah Jewels in India. He told us to bring back the quiver."

"Yes, well, how do you think he's going to feel when he learns that Jasmin is helping them," Slim replied. "He's going to be pretty angry about that, right?"

"Not as mad as he's going to be at us. I really don't think we have a chance. Might as well go face our fate," Moe sighed.

The pairs finished their refreshing drinks and began the hike out of the medina to their boss's house at the edge of the city. They entered through the side, making sure to avoid seeing any of the servants. They ducked past the kitchen, making sure to skip past the lady of the house undetected.

They turned the corner of the upstairs hallway, and Slim ran smack into Idrees, who was rounding the corner. "You two!" He exclaimed. "What are you doing here? Go to my study right now!"

The two young men walked to the older man's study and began to pace back and forth. Idrees, followed them in, sat behind his desk, and took a deep breath.

"I'm sure you have something to give me," Idrees said in a low tone.

"Boss, look, before we explain, I just want to say," Slim began before Idrees flicked his wrist and put his hand up, signalling to Slim to stop.

"You have nothing for me. You have been defeated by the Jannah Jewels. Again. Again," Idrees muttered, shaking his head, "you disappoint me. Again you fail me. Again they take an artifact to the clock."

Moe and Slim stood in front of their boss, heads hanging and hands limp at their sides. They had no defense - they had failed their master. Moe and Slim took turns explaining the mishap with the poisoned juice in India, and how Hidayah had won the competition by explaining the Qur'anic passage given to her by the Master Archer.

"Of course," Idrees reflected. "They outsmart you at every turn. They have fortune and blessings on their side because they contemplate Allah's word and live by His commands. Hidayah is not just learning to master the bow. She is also learning to master her faith and her belief in the wisdom of Allah."

"Faith, gentlemen. You don't have enough. You don't listen to Allah's will. The Jannah Jewels do. You need more focus and more faith if you are going to

14

disrupt their plans. And you must disrupt their plans," Idrees growled, his heart picking up pace.

Idrees closed his eyes. His mind wandered back to his youth, when he was the age of Jaffar and Jasmin. He had been training in archery his entire childhood, along with several of his classmates. As hard as Idrees worked, though, he never could beat his brother Khan, who was two years younger. Idrees worried about losing to his brother, but he worried even more about defeating his brother and causing distance between them.

The day before the Archery Battle, Idrees grew panicked and overwhelmed. When it was time for the competition, he disappeared, reading in the gardens behind his home. Rather than face the prospect of losing, he told everyone that he did not wish to compete.

When his brother lost to Layla, Idrees was torn. On the one hand, he was thankful that he did not lose to a woman. On the other hand, he believed he could have beaten her if he had been braver. The young and beautiful Layla would not need to take the title Idrees had worked for his entire life; he had basically given it to her.

But even though Khan had lost the Archery Battle, he had won the heart of Layla. Khan explained to his older brother that the two would be getting married. Idrees' heart broke a second time. Not only did Layla steal a title Idrees deserved, but she was causing the very distance he had feared. Idrees resolved once and for all to take the title of Master Archer away from Layla and hold it himself, as he had always felt deserved to do.

Idrees opened his eyes and returned to the present. "You only have two more chances. They have ten - ten - of the artifacts! Time is short. You will need to go back in time again and confront them."

He reached in front of his desk and unlocked a small, hidden drawer. Within it was a scroll, which he removed and unrolled to reveal a tattered, faded map. Idrees ran his fingers over the ink, and took a deep breath. Again, he closed his eyes.

Idrees wandered back through his mind to the last summer before Layla fled her family. Idrees had built his house in Fes near Khan's, and the families were close. Layla often left her family for days at a time to fulfill her duties as a Master Archer. While she was away, Idrees would sneak into her study and read her books on archery, hoping to improve his skills.

It was during this summer that he learned about the great clock, into which Layla had locked away a great secret given to her by the previous Archer. Yet in all her papers and notes within her study, Idrees could find no mention of what the secret was, simply that it was of vital importance for the Master Archer to protect it.

What he did find was a map with twelve locations marked on it. Each spot was marked with the name of an object. Idrees could not understand the strange map, but there was a strong sense within him that this map was important for the Master Archer's plans.

On one hot August night, Idrees and Nur, his wife, were visiting the family. The families sat around the garden fountains, drinking sweet tangerine juice and telling stories to the children. Idrees stole away and snuck upstairs to Layla's study. He quickly made a copy of the map, and tucked it away into his jacket pocket. Though he did not understand then what the map would be for, he knew it would be useful someday in the future.

Idrees opened his eyes and studied the map carefully. He knew where the girls had picked up artifacts from the reports Moe and Slim had given him. He suspected one of the Jewels was carrying Layla's copy of the map. He had been tracking the Jewels the entire time, on each of their missions, studying their progress. "There are only two locations left that have not been visited by the Jannah Jewels. Here," Idrees pointed to a spot marked in Central Asia.

"And Egypt," Idrees concluded, nodding his head. "Both of the remaining locations have Mamluk artifacts, so the Jewels will be going to Egypt, where the Mamluks ruled."

"We'll go get Jaffar," Slim chimed in. "He can help us defeat Jasmin and the girls."

"Jasmin?" Idrees' voice hit a high note. "She is

helping the Jewels? She must have met her mother, and been turned to their cause." He shook his head in disappointment. "She must be considered a liability now. She will be a good bit of help to the Jewels. And we can't trust Jaffar. I fear he and Khan have softened. Their love for Layla has been too strong."

"I had always hoped that their love would pull them together," Idrees said, shaking his head in frustration. "But I had hoped it would draw Layla away from her duties as Master Archer, not draw the rest of the family to the clock."

"No," Idrees concluded. "Jaffar cannot be trusted. You two will have to complete this task for me alone. I cannot impress upon you enough how important these last two artifacts are. We need leverage. We need some way to negotiate to get the clock open. Now go. Go to Egypt and get me the artifact they seek. You must stop them."

"Even Jasmin?" Moe asked in shock. "Even your own niece?"

"Even Jasmin," Idrees responded, his mind already wandering to his past. "She will not hesitate to help the Jannah Jewels. She is no longer my ally."

Moe and Slim ducked out through the open doorway and shut the door behind them. Idrees held his head in his hands and sighed. The great Archery Battle was coming up, and he could not depend on knowing the secret in the golden clock. At least, he hoped, he could prevent Hidayah, Jaffar, or Jasmin from knowing it.

He had to continue to study for the battle. Surely, with all his years of experience, he would finally be able to win the battle and take the title of Master Archer, as he had deserved so many years ago. Layla could return to her family, and finally, all his plans would come to fruition.

He looked down to the archery manuscript he was studying. Still, his stomach felt uneasy. The future was very unclear. "If only Moe and Slim could actually accomplish their task," Idrees muttered to himself...

Moe and Slim stepped away from the door, and looked at one another. They didn't speak a word because they didn't need to - both knew that they could not afford to make any more mistakes. Slim walked off, with Moe right behind, leaving the hallway empty.

Suddenly, the curtain across the hall from the door to Idrees' room stirred. The hallway was not so empty after all. Jaffar poked his head around the curtain, checking to make sure there was no one who could see him. He stepped out and stood in the hall, staring at the door to Idrees' room.

Jaffar felt so much anger in his heart. He had heard everything Idrees had said. How could Idrees speak so ill of him, and of his father, Khan? His father was Idrees' own younger brother. Everyone in the family trusted Idrees.

The betrayal took Jaffar's breath away. All these years, while he was separated from his mother, it was because Idrees had tricked his parents. All the times Idrees acted like a father figure to him, it was all part of a plan to take his mother's position as Master Archer.

Jaffar raised his hand into a fist, ready to bang on the door. He would confront his Uncle Idrees.

But before he could knock, he stopped, fist in mid air. He reflected on his calligraphy and painting. He remembered that all things must come in time, and that patience and discipline were virtues he must develop if he wanted to be a talented archer or painter.

Jaffar realized that his father had been betrayed more than anyone by his Uncle Idrees. His father needed to confront Idrees and learn the full truth. As angry as Jaffar was, he was still a young man, and he knew he had to leave such monumental matters to men of experience. He dropped his fist, and took a deep breath.

He had only one choice. He ran down the hall, out of the house, and back toward his father's house. Khan had to learn what his brother had done.

3

Sands of the Past

They looked at the two remaining artifact markers on the map.

MAMLUK ENAMELLED LAMP

Egypt, North Africa

MAMLUK ORNATE TRUNK

Uzbekistan, Central Asia

"Well, Egypt is one of the two remaining locations, so we really are in the Sahara!" Jaide exclaimed. "But how are we to know when we are?"

"Look at this," Jasmin said, her brow furrowing and her eyes squinting. "Both artifacts are Mamluk. But North Africa... and Central Asia. Aren't these artifacts from very different parts of the world? How are they both Mamluk?"

Iman leaned back away from the map, and pulled out her Book of Knowledge. She motioned for the girls to wrap the map back up, and Hidayah put it back in her bag as Iman put the book out in front of the group. She opened it up to the page on the Mamluks.

"Let me see," Iman began. "Looks to me like the Mamluks were one of the great Islamic dynasties to rule many of the lands of North Africa and the Middle East. Their leaders were slaves who became knights and served across many territories. They ruled for nearly a millennia in various places, and ruled Egypt for about 250 years, from 1250 - 1500. They were very successful militarily…"

"My goodness, there's a lot here. I don't even know what to focus on," Iman said, confused.

Hidayah interrupted, "Well, does your book say anything about lamps or trunks… or Uzbekistan."

Iman kept reading. "Oh, wait," she said with a happier voice. "It does say here that, under the

Mamluks, artists in Egypt made beautiful metalwork house goods. It also says that they were well-known for their skillfully made enamelled glass, and that this glass would be traded across the Mamluk's empire, including Africa, the Middle East, Central Asia, and all the way to India."

"Well, that would include Uzbekistan, right? So the Mamluks were in Egypt, but had trade relations with the Uzbeks. And the Mamluks would make that glass and that trunk here in Egypt. Maybe that's how all this is connected?" Sara pondered.

"This is all great, but we have no idea where we are, other than knowing it's the Sahara of Egypt. Which, if I remember correctly," Jasmin warned, "is a giant desert that lots of people get lost in. I would love to read all day, but this could be dangerous. We need a plan."

"Don't worry!" Jaide was already on her feet, running off to edge of the dune. She climbed up to the top, got out her skateboard, and began rolling up and down the dunes like a halfpipe. "I've got a plan!" she yelled.

As Jaide rolled from dune to dune, she gained speed, launching herself higher and higher into the air in various directions. After about a minute, she ran back to the girls, out of breath.

"There," she pointed off in one direction, panting. "There! I saw the city over there, just over a few dunes. Maybe a mile off. Maybe two. But not that far. A big city, lots of buildings." She continued to pant. "Whew! That was tiring! Can I have a drink, Sara?"

Sara ran over and gave Jaide her canteen. Jaide took a big sip, catching her breath in the hot sun.

"Fantastic! Any chance you have a snack?" Jaide asked, half joking.

The girls laughed heartily, happy to have an idea of where to go. They began the short trek to the city. As they walked, however, the short distance seemed to stretch as the desert sun made them hot and tired. Finally, they reached the edge of the city, finding a row of stables for travellers to stable their camels.

"Camel humps!" Iman suddenly yelled, and the girls looked wearily at a trio of camels tied to a post on the edge of the stables. "The riddle! We're supposed to get over the hump! It must be a camel!"

"But which one? And where are we going?" Jasmin shook her head. "We can't just say, 'take us to a lamp' and the camel will know where to go."

"Miss! Oh Miss!" A little old man wrapped in a navy cloak with a bright orange headscarf wrapped around his head ran toward them. "All my young ladies! Do you need a ride?"

The man motioned toward his camels, which looked strong and healthy. Iman walked over and began petting the first camel, who rubbed his head against her cheek and blinked his giant eyelashes at the girls.

"I want this one!" Iman cheered. "He is very happy. These camels seem well-cared for and healthy. We can certainly ride them to our next destination."

"My guides, they can take you to the pyramids. You want to go to the pyramids, right? And to see the mighty Sphinx!" The old man was warm and inviting. He motioned to the camels, and his working boys began fitting 5 camels with saddles for the girls.

"Perhaps 'following our noses' in the riddle means we should go see the Sphinx," Hidayah argued, "that famous statue that's missing its nose. It seems like as good idea as any other."

The girls began packing their bags tight, and they helped the working boys to get the saddles ready. The old man walked back into his stable office and called over his two guides.

"Alright, boys, I don't know what you're doing, but I did as you asked," the old man said. Moe handed the man a small bag of gold.

"You told them the pyramids, right? And the Sphinx, just like we asked?" Slim asked in a hushed tone. "You told them the guides would take them, right?"

"Yes! Yes!" the old man whispered in an angry tone. "I don't understand at all. But I did as you asked. Now go, and leave me. I do not like this at all, and if I didn't need your money, I wouldn't help you. I can tell you have a terrible plan for those girls. Get out of here before I change my mind!"

"Take your gold, old man. Do not judge us. Our

master is a good man, and our mission is honorable," Moe growled at the man, who cringed in disgust. The pair pulled their hoods, navy and black, over their heads, hiding their faces. They pulled on gloves to hide their hands, becoming unrecognizable.

The two dark guides walked out to the camels, which were lined up in a caravan line, each crowned with one of the Jannah Jewels. Hidayah rode in the front, while Jasmin guarded the rear.

"Are you ready, girls?" Moe called out in a high, squeaky tone that hid his real identity. The dark guides walked out into the desert, leading the string of camels behind them, while the girls cheered and chatted, enjoying the view of the dunes.

"This is so much better than walking on the dunes," Iman called out. She patted her camel on his head. "You're such a great help, my friend!"

The girls chatted and joked, enjoying the slow and steady pace of the camel ride. Sitting on top of the humps, the girls rocked back and forth as the camels' long legs dragged the line up and down the dunes. After a while, the two guides circled the camels and motioned for the girls to wait. Each camel sat on his knees, and each Jannah Jewel jumped off her camel's back.

"I don't see any pyramids," Jaide remarked. "They're… they're supposed to be pretty big, right?"

"Oh, mistress, they are over the dunes there, a short walk. Look," the guide in black pointed past the dunes, and the girls could make out the tips of the stone pyramids. "They are out there. But the camels cannot go too close. There are many loose stones and they hurt the camels' soft feet."

"We will wait here," the guide in blue continued, "and when you are finished with your quest, return here. We will take you back to the city. The camels will rest."

The girls each looked at other and nodded. After all, they each thought, there was no reason to hurt the feet of their wonderful transport. Iman walked over to her camel and rubbed his face.

"I'll be back soon," she whispered. But the camel looked at her with tears in his eyes, on his long eyelashes. He rubbed his head against her shoulder, pushing her back toward his saddle. Iman shook her head. "No, my friend, I'll be back soon. Do not worry." As she walked away, the camel let out a high cry, as if he was trying to warn her.

4

Hidden Pharaohs

The girls walked over the dune and started the short hike to the pyramids. Within 10 minutes, they reached the base of the first pyramid.

"Ummmm... how are we here already? I thought these were huge," Sara said with some disappointment.

"It was a mirage," Jasmin exclaimed. "A mirage is a trick of the eye that the desert plays. We expected the pyramids to be huge, so our eyes told us they were far away. But they are smaller, and our eyes played tricks. But..." she paused, "but I did expect them to be bigger."

"And where is the Sphinx? Is this some trick?"

Sara asked with frustration. The girls began running from the first pyramid to the second, which was taller. Hidayah began climbing to the top, and other girls followed. The girls stood on the giant rock at the top of the middle pyramid, looking at the action a short distance beneath them. Iman sat and pulled out her Book of Knowledge, and began to read to herself as the other girls starting chatting about the scene.

From the top, the girls could see a handful of young men with hammers, pulling a smooth, shiny white stone off the third pyramid. As the girls watched, the men tore the stone off and began the long process of dragging it away in the direction of the city.

"Look over there," Jaide pointed to a giant head, sitting in a dune of sand beneath them. "It's the head of the Sphinx. Just his head, though. But he has his nose! This makes no sense."

"Wait," Iman interrupted. "It does. It does make sense. It all makes sense!" Her voice filled with excitement as the other girls turned to face her.

"I started reading about the pyramids, to see if

I could understand what we see here. You see, the pyramids are already over 3,000 years old, even now. But after the pharaohs disappeared in Egypt, no one used the pyramids. Egypt became Christian, then Muslim. And the pyramids and Sphinx, they became buried in the sand over time."

"Buried? You mean these pyramids are buried?" Hidayah asked.

"Oh course!" Jasmin cheered. "It's not that the pyramids are too small. We are only seeing the top half of them! The bottom half is buried in the sands. So each pyramid is only the top of the monument."

"That's right!" Iman continued. "The pyramids are actually hundreds of feet taller than we see. Hundreds of tons of rock are buried beneath these sands. It would not be until the 1800s that anyone would dig these pyramids out of the sand and study them. During this time, the people did not even know why these buildings were here."

"Time travel is confusing," Jaide said, shaking her head.

"In fact, it says in the book that the Mamluks

actually came out to the buried pyramids and cleared out some of the sand so that they could see the shiny white limestone that covered the outside of the pyramids." Iman explained, "the Mamluks would tear off pieces of the beautiful limestone to use in building their own buildings."

"But the pyramids aren't white!" Sara said with great doubt. "I've seen photos back in Vancouver. The pyramids are made of sandy yellow stone."

"Well, in our future they are!" Iman confirmed. "But when the pharaohs built them thousands of years ago, the pyramids were actually bright white, covered in shiny limestone. The Mamluks stole it all! They changed the way all of humanity saw the pyramids. We're watching history in progress, standing in the middle."

"No," Sara disagreed, "they didn't steal. The pharaohs were long gone. The Mamluks recycled. Instead of ruining more nature by digging up new stones, they recycled. Sounds pretty smart to me!"

"Either way, it looks to me like the Sphinx down there has his nose. Did the Mamluks recycle that

36

too?" Jasmin asked.

"Oh, no. It says here that the Sphinx didn't lose his nose until that French General Napoleon, hundreds of years from now," Iman replied.

"Wow. It's like all of history is relative. We have to remember that all things change over time - friendships, family, stone monuments, stories," Jasmin said wistfully. "We never even realized that we were stepping into the large historical flows of each time and place we visit. Think of all the moments you, Jannah Jewels, have witnessed snapshots of different moments in human history."

"Good thing you've got your nose in your book, Iman," Sara joked. "We might not have been able to reflect on all that we are seeing here. Hey! Maybe the nose, in the riddle that we are supposed to follow, is yours, my friend."

Iman laughed. "I suppose it's my nose after all. Makes more sense that way since people during this time period would not have even known that the Sphinx really existed. All they'd see is some old head in the sand."

"Then… wait…" Hidayah said in a frightened tone. "If locals in this time don't know about the Sphinx, how did the man who gave us the camels know about the Sphinx?" Hidayah's mind started turning and pondering. "How did he know where to send us?"

Hidayah jumped forward, and began to run down the side of the pyramid at top speed. The other girls followed her, stumbling. They dropped onto the sand, and Hidayah began running full speed. As the girls ran, each became more worried at Hidayah's rush back to the camels.

They reached the top of the dune, and suddenly Hidayah came to a halt. The girls caught up, huffing and puffing. They looked down at the space below where the camels and their two guides were waiting.

It was completely empty. The camels were gone, and their guides were nowhere to be seen.

"The man renting us the camels was told where to send us," Hidayah said. "He was told by someone from our time who made a mistake, we just didn't catch it soon enough. Someone who wanted to lead us out here. Someone who wanted to set a trap. And it worked."

The girls shook their heads in disbelief. How could they have been so foolish? They were alone on the dunes, no camels, no water, no help. They decided to sit in a circle and pray for guidance, then formulate some kind of plan.

They closed their eyes, and began to pray. "Allah, the Merciful, the Compassionate, guide us in this hour of dire need," Hidayah began. The girls tried to calm their hearts and clear their minds so that they could find some solution to their dilemma.

"Iman, stop tickling my back!" Sara suddenly said. "I'm praying!"

"I'm not doing anything!" Iman snapped back. "Is it the wind?" She leaned back and looked behind Sara.

"Oh! My! It looks like you've made a little friend! How did you sneak up on us?" Iman asked, looking at a small black cat sitting on the sand behind Sara, pawing at her back. The cat hopped to his feet and strolled over to Iman. She sat down between Iman's

legs and rubbed his face up against Iman's chest, beginning to purr.

"Of course," Hidayah said, shaking her head. "The Prophet's most favorite animal, Muezza. Just as the riddle foretold."

"Most favorite?" Jaide asked, confused.

"Yes. One of my most favorite stories of Muhammad (pbuh)," Iman noted while rubbing the cat on his belly. The cat purred and played happily. "The Prophet, peace and blessings be upon him, awoke and prepared for morning prayers. When he went to put on his prayer robe, he found his cat Muezza asleep on the sleeve. Muhammad took out his blade and cut the sleeve off, so that he would not disturb his beloved Muezza."

"Indeed. Cats are so helpful, keeping away rats and mice that carry disease. They are important for the environment," Sara noted.

"And they are smart," Iman finished. "They can see in the dark and navigate deserts and cities. They are great companions. Perhaps this one will help us. Can you help us, little Muezza?" As she said this, the cat took to his feet, and walked away from the girls, down the side of the dune.

The girls heard him meow loudly. They stood, and climbed down the dune, where Muezza stood expectantly. As soon as they caught up, he trotted off again. They began to follow him through the desert.

"Are you sure we should be following a cat through the Sahara?" Jasmin asked hesitantly.

"Well," Hidayah said, her voice betraying her fear and uncertainty, "do you have any better ideas?"

5

Muezza

The nimble little cat scrambled up and down the dunes, trotting at an even pace so the girls could keep up with him.

"This seems so easy for him," Iman complained, out of breath from struggling up the walls of sand.

Sara replied, "he's a desert cat. His body is in tune with desert. See how he flattens out his paws really wide when he steps down, so that his feet can grip the sand? That way, he has more traction and can climb on the sand easier. His whiskers can smell food from miles away in the hot, dry air. And even his eyes are special so that he can see well in the dark, desert nights, when the dunes are lit only by the moon."

"Well, Allah has built the cat to be a master of the desert it seems," Jaide joked. "Look at how quickly he has helped us!"

Jaide pointed ahead of her, and off in the distance, the girls could see what looked like a large collection of tents, with many hazy figures running back and forth. All the figures wore dark crimson robes with heavy leather belts.

The girls jogged behind Muezza, who led them forward with his head held high. As the girls approached the encampment, a tall, reedy young man barely older than them ran up.

"Hello, ladies. How strange to see five young women walking out of the desert, all alone. No camels, no men to help. Are you alright?" he asked in a voice that showed genuine concern.

"We need no men to help us! We're just fine on our own!" Jaide snapped back in an angry tone. "How do you know we are not here to attack you all?"

"Jaide!" Hidayah chastised her companion.

"There's no need to threaten this soldier!"

"No worries, young mistress. I was not threatened by you, not because you are women, but because you have marched out of the desert. Surely the heat has exhausted you. How could you attack an entire camp of Mamluk soldiers, the best in all of Africa and Asia, with only the five of you?"

"And a cat," Iman confirmed. "We also have a cat." Muezza meowed loudly in agreement.

"Thank you for your concern!" Sara chimed in, clearly annoyed that her companions were so distracted. "We have been lost in the desert, and would love to refill our canteens and use your assistance. We were riding camels in the dunes, you see, but our guides stole our camels and abandoned us."

"Well, let me take you to my boss, Commander Abdullah, and he can provide you with anything you need. Be our guests," the young soldier motioned for the Jewels to follow him. Muezza walked beside the man, his eyes peeled for danger.

The young soldier brought the girls deep into

the camp, and led them to a tall, stocky man with broad shoulders and a commanding presence. Commander Abdullah greeted the girls, and then stood listening to the young soldier explain their plight. He nodded his head.

"Come, my guests. We will help you out of course. Please follow me to my tent, where you can eat and drink to your fill," the Commander's voice, though strong, was pleasant and friendly. "All these men around us are my Mamluk soldiers, and will host you graciously." The group began to walk through the camp, where many soldiers were practicing fighting skills.

"Would you look at them," Jasmin tapped Hidayah on the arm, then pointed to a trio of young men standing, blindfolded, and firing arrows at targets. "They practice with their eyes covered."

"Sensei Elle had me do it once. It was incredibly hard," Hidayah said, nodding. "I can't imagine practicing that way all day."

"Yes, our archers train so that they can shoot under any condition. Sometimes, night can be dark,

so they must know how to aim without using their eyes," Commander Abdullah explained.

"What are those men doing over there?" Jaide asked, pointing to a pack of young soldiers sitting with maps on their laps, listening to a older man lecture.

"They are some of our scouts. They receive special education in drawing and reading maps so that they can gather information for us when they go out on missions." Commander Abdullah picked up one of the maps and showed the girls. "These maps show the environmental conditions and the locations of settlements."

"These are beautiful!" Jaide exclaimed.

"And I think it's great that they gather information on the environment. Understanding nature better will make them better soldiers," Sara argued.

The girls continued their stroll through the camp with the Commander, asking questions and observing the Mamluks various military activities. Iman noted that the men serving under Commander Abdullah seemed very diverse.

"Yes. Our empire is different than others. The Mamluks are the soldiers who fight for the leader. We are born all over the empire, and come from many tribes and races. When we are young boys, we join the military and get expert training, like you see around you," Commander Abdullah motioned around him.

"When our Sultan dies, we do not pass the power on father to son. Rather, we choose from the military. This makes our leadership based on merit, not family. And it means that anyone in the empire can lead, no matter his background, if he works hard enough."

Jasmin sighed softly. Deep, in the back of her mind, she had always assumed that, because her mother was the Master Archer, that she was destined to be the next Master. She had always assumed that only Jaffar, also a child of Layla, could take that position away from Jasmin. She felt like it was hers by right. But listening to the Mamluks' story, she began to think differently about the position of Master Archer.

Who was to say that it had to pass from mother to

child? Perhaps bringing in an outsider to take the role next would be better. Jasmin realized she had been too proud, and too vain, assuming that she should automatically be given the position, not because of skill but because of heritage. She resolved to earn the position of Master Archer by winning the Archery Battle through talent, or to be happy for Hidayah if she defeated her.

But the Jannah Jewels interpreted Commander Abdullah's story differently. The Mamluks succeeded in history because they brought outsiders into the group, who had new skills and ideas. As much as they had enjoyed their adventures together finding the first few artifacts, the most recent travels had been full of dangers, and Jasmin had become a valuable member of the team. The Jewels realized that their new companion had earned herself a spot among them through skill and loyalty.

"But, my friends, if you are hoping to learn more about leadership and authority, you ought to speak to the great scholar of Al Azhar, Ibn Khaldun," the Commander said encouragingly. "And if you are going to do so, perhaps you could do me a favor?"

"Of course, Commander," Hidayah reassured him. "You have been a generous host, so we would love to help out if we can."

"Wonderful! My friend Ibn Khaldun recently bought a chest, and the key was cracked. He gave it to me to have my military blacksmith fix it," Commander Abdullah explained. "I need to return it to him, but he's across Cairo at Al Azhar and I'm too busy. Since you need to speak with him anyway, please deliver his silver key back to him with my well wishes."

"I'll hand it to him personally, Commander," Jaide assured him, taking the key and placing it in her jacket. "Perhaps you could answer one more question for us? Would you know where we could get an enameled lamp?"

"Oh, my. Well, most homes have them. And they are in mosques and schools." Commander Abdullah paused and thought deeply. "But if you are looking for the most beautiful, ornate, and sacred enameled lamps, I would go to the holy Mosque of Sultan Hassan. There are magnificent lamps hanging there."

"So what do we do next?" Sara asked. "We've got to deliver this key to Ibn Khaldun over at... where did you say again?"

What the girls did not realize was that, just outside their tent, two hooded figures congratulated each other, and far off in the market, a cat was leaping out of a sack and fleeing.

6

Jumpy Cat

The two hooded figures snuck back to the camel herder's stable, tying the camels to the post. They scurried away, walking along the edge of the soldiers' camps that bordered Cairo's perimeter. They grabbed a seat on a stone near a trio of tents, and huddled their heads together.

"Alright," Moe whispered, 'that has got to be enough! We left them in the middle of the desert, with no water, and no map! There is simply no way they will come back."

"They're going to die, you know, from exhaustion or dehydration," Slim shook his head. "I don't know if that was wrong. Maybe we were too extreme."

"Slim, stop. Idrees gave us a mission. We have tried everything. We tried distracting them. What about in India when we poisoned them? Still, they succeeded at obtaining the artifact and defeating us. No," Moe growled, "we must have a foolproof plan."

"Fine. Yes. We must not fail the boss again. I understand," Slim muttered.

Suddenly, a small black cat trotted down the path near them, head high and whiskers flopping in the breeze. Behind him was a gaggle of girls, goofing around, laughing and smiling as they followed the cat.

"This is some kind of joke," Moe gasped, his voice in shock. "They survived the desert!"

"Are you kidding?" Slim squeezed his fists in anger. "And I felt bad we were so cruel to them! But we weren't! We cannot defeat them! How did they get here from the desert? This is madness!"

The dark pair watched as the slender cat weaved his way through the crowds, and the girls traced his path.

"The cat, Moe. I can't believe it," Slim muttered,

"but it looks like they are following that cat. Perhaps he was sent by Allah to save them. That must be it. He must be a blessed cat, to protect them and lead them."

"That's crazy talk, Slim, and I won't believe it. It must be luck. Look - if they are following the cat, we'll just take the cat. It's a cat, for goodness' sake! How hard can it be to steal a cat?"

"Moe, I don't know. How hard was it to leave five girls in the desert? I just don't know…" Slim trailed off.

"Come, my friend. He's just a cat. You wait here, and I'll grab him right up, and those girls will be lost without a clue," Moe said reassuringly.

Moe and Slim followed the Jannah Jewels as the girls walked with Commander Abdullah, asking questions about the military training. Muezza pranced along behind the girls, acting like he didn't have a care in the world.

Slim jogged past the path where the girls were standing, listening to the Commander, and as he swept past Muezza, he quietly reached down and scooped the cat up. Slim stuffed Muezza in the belt of his pants and pretended nothing had happened.

Without warning, Muezza tucked his ears back and hunched his body together and wiggled his way down into Slim's pants. Since Slim was so skinny, there was just enough room for Muezza to squeeze down the leg of Slim's pants and escape. All Moe saw was Slim suddenly leap into the air and yelp like he had been stung by a bee, shaking his pants out. Muezza scrambled off, running back to the girls who were now asking about lectures being held.

Sara, Jaide, and Iman did not even notice Moe sneak through the back row of students studying maps and grab Muezza, who had ducked under the legs of one student. Moe ran back to Slim, holding Muezza with his fat, meaty fingers. He jammed the poor companion under his arm like a sack of potatoes.

But before Moe could get back to the corner where Slim was standing, Muezza curled himself up under Moe's arm and crawled up his back. He hopped on Moe's turban and jumped off his head to

the canopy of a nearby food cart. Muezza sped up the rope holding up the canopy, ran across the top of a pair of buildings, and dropped down next to Iman, rubbing against her leg.

Moe cursed under his breath. Clearly, he and Slim were going to have to work together to capture this crafty cat.

As the girls began walking, Muezza stopped and lifted his nose in the air. Fish! That was definitely fish! He looked to the left and saw a man wrapped in dark blue robes holding out a fish and beckoning him. Muezza was awfully hungry, so he trotted over to the figure in blue, and began gnawing on the fish the man held.

Suddenly, a hand reached out and grabbed Muezza behind his head. The hand picked Muezza up and wrapped him up in a heavy cloak.

"Quick! Oh, please, do not delay! We've got to get him in a chest or a box or something! He's too crafty." Slim moaned.

Moe ran over to a nearby tent, and found a small trunk full of buckles. He dumped them on the ground, and grabbed the trunk, carrying it over to Slim. The cat was screeching and jumping, but Slim had him wrapped up in the cloak and so the cat could not escape.

"Alright, Slim. On three, put the cat and the cloak in the trunk, and I'll shut the top. Then he can't escape. One, two…" Moe counted.

On three, Slim shoved the cloak and cat into the trunk, and Moe snapped it shut. They could hear the cat bouncing around inside, clawing at the lid. Slim looked through the keyhole. Suddenly, he could see the eye of the cat looking through the keyhole back at him, and the two stared at each other. The cat growled and hissed inside, but waited frustratedly.

Moe picked up the trunk and ran to the nearest soldier. He explained to the soldier that Commander Abdullah ordered for the cat inside to be sold off deep in the market, but that they did not have time. The young soldier took the trunk, then shook his head.

"How do I know the Commander told you to sell this cat?" the young soldier asked.

"Oh, my friend has a note from him. It's in his

cloak! Slim," Moe motioned to Slim, "give him the letter!"

"Well, Moe, my cloak is in the trunk. We stuck it in when we captured the cat." Slim responded, winking a little at Moe. The young man fell for the trick.

"If you open the trunk," Moe warned, "the cat will run away, and then the Commander will be angry at you. What you should do is sell the cat, and when the customer opens the trunk, take the cloak. Then you can read the letter from the Commander."

"Fair enough," the young soldier agreed. "I will do that. And if you are lying, I will keep the cloak and the money!"

"Hey - don't steal my cloak!" Slim yelled, and Moe stamped on Slim's foot to silence him.

"That won't be a problem," Moe responded, "because, of course, the letter is inside! Now hurry! Run! That cat should have been sold already. The Commander will want a report as soon as you are done!"

The young soldier nodded, picked up the trunk,

and looked through the keyhole. The cat looked back through, and made a whining sound. The soldier stood, shrugged, and ran off into the bazaar with the trunk. Moe and Slim looked at each other, smiling, and pulled their hoods over their heads, hiding their faces, Then they snuck into the crowd of soldiers, and disappeared from view.

*   *   *   *   *

The girls wandered through the camp. Many young men were honing their craft. Some were practicing their archery, others their riding skills. Even young boys ran around with dull swords and little wood shields, practicing basic moves. When the girls followed the Commander into the tent, they chatted, and then he gave them the silver key.

"So what do we do next?" Sara asked. "We've got to deliver this key to Ibn Khaldun over at... where did you say again?"

"Al-Azhar," Commander Abdullah repeated. "He is giving a lecture in history at the great university of Al-Azhar across Cairo."

Jasmin nodded. "Then we will take the key over

to him, as you have asked."

"Sara and I can take the key to Ibn Khaldun at the university. We can ride over on my skateboard," Jaide suggested. "You three follow the cat to the Mosque to pick up the lamp."

"A great idea!" Hidayah cheered. "So, dear feline friend, which direction should we… wait… Iman? Where is the cat?"

Iman looked around the tent. "He's not here. He's gone!"

Suddenly, a young soldier ran into the tent, out of breath. "Commander! I think I have been tricked!"

"Catch your breath, young man! Tell us what has happened!" the Commander ordered.

"Well, you see, sir, there were these two men. They had this trunk, with a cat, and told me to sell it. They said it was on your orders, Commander Abdullah, but it was a trick," the young soldier tried to catch his breath.

The Commander shook his head, "You fool! You sold the trunk? Or the cat? Or both?"

"Well," the soldier continued, "I sold the cat inside the trunk, but when the man opened the trunk, the cat leapt out and fled. I had to give the man the trunk as a gift because I sold him a missing cat!"

"He had shredded that poor cape up too," the young soldier finished. A hooded man standing in the back of the tent coughed loudly. His companion elbowed him in the ribs, and the pair fell silent. Then they slipped out the back as everyone turned their attention to Hidayah.

"Then we'll have to go to the bazaar and find our cat!" she yelled. "We have to do that first before we deliver the key or pick up the lamp!"

"I am so sorry, my friends," the Commander apologized to the girls. He looked at his soldier. "This kind of mistake won't happen again, will it?"

"Of course! I mean," the young soldier stuttered, "I mean of course it won't happen again! Come! Let me take you to the bazaar, and show you the last place I saw the cat. Maybe he will not have gone far!"

The five girls grabbed their bags. They each

took a turn giving salaam to the Commander, and thanked them for the lessons. They promised to return the key to Ibn Khaldun. They walked out of the tent, following the young soldier.

"So," Sara asked as they began walking deep into the city of Cairo, "what is sold at this bazaar?"

The young soldier turned to the girls, bewildered. "Have you never been to the great Cairo bazaar? It is not a question of what is sold at the Cairo bazaar."

He motioned down into the streets in front of him, packed with stalls and hundreds of shoppers.

"The question is, instead: what isn't sold at the Cairo bazaar?"

7

A Very Super Market

In front of them, the girls looked out on a chaotic scene. Stalls featured gold jewelry, piles of spices and sacks of dried flowers, paintings and calligraphy, copper pots, glass goblets, parakeets, sponges and brushes, chessboards, and more. Every turn revealed a new crowd of vendors and customers, haggling over prices and weights.

"Alright ladies," Hidayah said, taking charge. "There's a lot of different things sold in this bazaar market here. We know Muezza was sold somewhere. He could be anywhere. Let's split up and look for him. Wander for 20 minutes into the market, then meet on the other side. If you find the cat, pick him up and bring him with you to the meeting point."

The girls each took a deep breath, and walked off into the bazaar. While it was a little scary to dive into the massive crowds, the girls were soon entranced by the seemingly endless stalls stretching before them, each offering some colorful collection of goods. The girls passed markets for many fascinating items - spices and herbs, shoes, gold jewelry, rugs and carpets, even exotic birds from across the Mamluk empire. The girls split up and began their own search.

Iman wandered into a cluster of shops, and she immediately recognized the smell of ink and parchment. Sure enough, each stall held stacks of books, each hand-painted. Iman walked to the first vendor, and began leafing through some of the manuscripts he had piled on a table. She then turned her attention to a series of maps he had piled on the table before moving to the next merchant.

Most of the manuscripts appeared to be in Arabic, but Iman also saw calligraphy in Greek and Hebrew. She was reminded that Cairo, like Alexandria had a thousand years earlier, served as a central location for scholars from around the world to meet and

study together. It only made sense that there would be books on sale in all sorts of languages. Still, the cat was not hiding in a book, and Iman was forced at each shop to abandon an interesting find and press on in the search for Muezza.

Sara strolled slowly into a darker, covered market. The air felt a little more damp, and she immediately felt at ease. Around her were plants of various kinds, from small potted herbs to stocky tomato vines. Many of the plants were small enough to be grown indoors, which made sense to Sara. She had been noticing how harsh and unforgiving the Sahara climate had been on their journey. In this market, residents of Cairo could buy the plants that would help keep their houses in tune with nature and their tables stocked with food. But as pleasant at the plant market felt, it did not seem to host the missing cat.

Jaide followed her nose, catching a quick whiff of the familiar scent of paints and charcoal. Just a block down from Iman's search in the book market, Jaide found the market full of artists. Painters worked on pictures for homes. Others created decorations with Qur'anic calligraphy beautifully glazed onto their surfaces, combining faith and artistry. Jaide took out her sketchbook and made small sketches of various pieces she admired, but kept her eye out for Muezza.

Jasmin followed a pack of young women, who were giggling and chatting while walking with purpose. They all reached a market selling fine cloth. Jasmin stared in amazement at the richly embroidered silks and satins covered with floral patterns and bright hues. The vendors displayed skeins of fabric in every color imaginable, as well as spools of matching threads to sew the fabrics into lovely clothes. Yet while Jasmin was almost overwhelmed by the rainbow of colors and power of feminine beauty, she kept her cool and looked high and low for the cat.

Hidayah searched high and low, walking quickly along the path and keeping her eyes peeled for any cats. Suddenly, she became aware of a loud series of clanging noises, and looked up. She had walked into the coppersmith's market within the bazaar, where people came to buy pots, pans, and other house goods. Young men beat copper kettles into shape while older men sold tea pots and lanterns to old women standing at each stall's front. No cats to be seen.

The five girls reached the far edge of the bazaar and met up with each other. None of them had found Muezza. The only market left was the leather market, which sat on the edge of the bazaar because of its strong smell. The girls walked into the market, and admired the stunning bags, shoes, and saddles on offer at each stall.

Suddenly, Jaide gasped. The other girls looked up, and followed her gaze to a small table on the edge of the market. Two heavy-set, sweaty men were focusing quite seriously on a game of backgammon being played between them. The first man moved his counter with his thick fingers, then reached over and grabbed a delicate pink tea glass, which he promptly emptied in one gulp. Curled in a ball underneath the table, fast asleep, was a handsome black cat.

"Muezza!" Iman hissed. "Please, my friend, come back to us and help us on our adventure." The cat opened his eyes and yawned an epic cat yawn. He rose to his feet and trotted over to the set of girls, rubbing his body against Iman's leg before sitting and licking his paw in front of them.

"Now we can continue," Hidayah announced. The girls nodded in agreement. Jaide pulled her skateboard out of her bag, and jumped on. Sara hopped on behind her and grabbed Jaide around her waist.

"We'll head to Al Azhar on my skateboard. Once there, we will deliver the key to Ibn Khaldun as Commander Abdullah asked," Jaide explained. "Come meet us there with the lamp once you get it at the Mosque Sultan Hassan."

Jasmin nodded, and Jaide tapped on her jacket pocket, where she was still holding the key the Commander had given her. Jaide skated off, with Sara along for the ride. The trio of girls turned to Muezza. The cat walked into the crowd, and Iman shrugged.

"Let's follow him. I'm sure he'll lead us to the Mosque of Sultan Hassan," Iman reassured Hidayah and Jasmin. The trio rushed to keep up with the nimble little cat as he weaved his way through the crowded bazaar toward the mosque.

8

Friend or Foe

Jaffar stormed into Khan's bedroom. "As salaamu alaikum dear Father, I must speak to you. I've learned something terrible. I need to know what we should do."

"Something terrible? Is this about your mother? Or sister?" Khan's face grew grave and concerned.

Jaffar took a deep breath, and then opened the floodgates to his mind. He told his father everything. He explained how he had worked with Moe and Slim to thwart the Jannah Jewels, but that he had not followed up on what the pair were doing once he began to work with the Jewels. He explained how he had stood outside his Uncle Idrees' door.

Then, Jaffar noticed as his father's face grew darker and pained as he continued. Jaffar repeated what he had heard Idrees say to Moe and Slim. He explained how the pair had been working for Idrees to ruin the plans of Layla and the Jannah Jewels. Then Jaffar warned his father that Moe and Slim had orders to go to Egypt to interfere with the mission of the Jannah Jewels.

"Jaffar, how could Idrees know where the Jannah Jewels are going next?"

Only the Master Archer would have that information. Someone would have to steal the Master Archer's map," Khan argued, shaking his head.

"Or copy it!" Jaffar countered. "He could have copied it, many years ago, before mother left us. Before she…" Jaffar's voice trailed off. "Before she abandoned us to fulfill her duties as the Master Archer."

"Jaffar, this all seems so hard to believe. I highly doubt that Idrees knows where the Jannah Jewels are going," Khan reassured him.

"That's not the worst of it, father," Jaffar objected.

"Idrees gave Moe and Slim, my own friends, the order to stop Jasmin and the Jewels. Do you understand father? Uncle Idrees told them that they could possibly hurt Jasmin if necessary to stop the Jewels from getting the last two artifacts. His own niece - your own daughter!"

"Enough! I command you, enough! I cannot believe such outrageous stories, about your Uncle no less! I am still your father," Khan bellowed at Jaffar, "and you will obey me! No more speaking ill of your Uncle Idrees! He has been a loyal younger brother to our family."

The two stared at each other in silence, breathing heavily. Jaffar realized that, though his father seemed older and frailer than he had in years past, there was still a fire in his eyes. Khan realized that, though his son still had much to learn, he had grown into a young man, strong and sure of his instincts.

"Am I interrupting something?" Idrees' voice suddenly cut into the room. A second later, Idrees entered, his head down as he read from a paper. "I hope I'm not. We must talk for a moment about the food for the Archery Battle next…"

Idrees' voice trailed off as he looked up and saw his brother and nephew staring at each other, bodies tense, jaws clenched. Idrees realized that, yes, indeed, he had interrupted something.

"I can go, my brother. I sense you and your son have words to share," Idrees said quietly as he slowly backed away.

"No, stay," Khan said, not moving a single hair on his body, still staring deep into his son's eyes. Neither man flinched. "Stay, Brother, and let us discuss the Battle tomorrow. We must make sure all our plans are sure and carried out successfully."

Idrees looked from one man to another. Neither father nor son moved or blinked. Idrees knew that he had interrupted something big. But there was nothing Idrees could do.

"Well, Aunt Nur needs the final numbers for the kitchen tonight, so that she can call the fish markets in Vancouver tomorrow and order the right amount of fish. It is the last ingredient she needs, fresh, and, well, you know how these women are… This is not important, I will leave you." Idress felt very uncomfortable, knowing that he was in the middle of a hurricane.

"I will send Mu'sab to her this evening," Jaffar said, breaking from his father's gaze and addressing his uncle. He turned his body toward Idrees.

"Mu'sab has been gathering the final counts of how many competitors and guests will arrive. We expect several hundred dignitaries and notables to come watch the Archery Battle. I will send Mu'sab to give her the most accurate numbers."

"Wonderful, Jaffar,' Idrees said as he smiled, "thank you so much. Your Aunt Nur is working so hard, and it is so good of you to be considerate of her feelings."

"Of course, Uncle Idrees," Jaffar said gently. "But we are not sure - do you think Jasmin will be competing? Or the Jannah Jewels? Will that be one or even two competitors to sit at the head table?"

Idrees shook his head, unsure of how to answer the question. Khan stayed silent, moving his gaze from his brother to his son and back again.

"I don't even know where they are," Jaffar tempted his uncle. "I don't even know where they are to ask them if they intend to compete."

"Well," Idrees responded, eager to end the awkward conversation, "I am sure when they get back from Egypt, they will tell you. I'm sure Hidayah will go to Vancouver, and Jasmin will come here. You'll have to ask them then."

"Yes, Uncle Idrees. Of course," Jaffar said slowly, closing his trap. "You are so wise. I'll ask when they get home from Egypt. And…"

Jaffar's eyes narrowed, "Wait a minute, how did you know they are in Egypt?"

Idrees stopped. No one knew he had the map except Moe and Slim. Had they told Jaffar? But when? When would they have had time? No, Idrees concluded, Jaffar must know some other way. Idrees began to panic.

"Well… I mean, they've been to so many different locations, from what you and Jasmin said. I'm surprised they haven't been to Egypt yet. That seems so likely." Idrees' voice cracked from the weakness of his lie. "How did you know they went to Egypt, Jaffar?"

"Oh, I didn't Uncle. I didn't know until you just confirmed it," Jaffar said methodically.

"Idrees," Khan's voice suddenly rang out, and both uncle and nephew turned toward Khan. "You have his answer, brother. Mu'sab will speak to Nur. Now, please, I am not well. My head is still weak. I must ask you to leave."

"Of course, brother!" Idrees smiled and sounded relieved to be given such a quick exit. "I will leave you to your rest. Nur thanks you all for your guidance."

Idrees left the room, closing the door behind him. Jaffar turned to his father.

"You know, father. You know that he is lying, and…" Jaffar began.

"Enough! I told you. I will hear no more of it. Leave me. My head hurts and I have found that I have grown very, very weary." Khan's voice was distant and tired.

"How I wish your mother was still here. She

always knew what to do."

*   *   *   *   *

That night, Khan could not sleep. He tossed and turned, alone in his bed. At times, he felt his heart swell up in his chest. He could not control his thoughts, and they bounced back and forth. He knew he could trust Jaffar. Yet he thought he could also trust Idrees. He had trusted his older brother his whole life.

Yet who was with them when the dark forces had attacked Khan's family all those years ago? He could barely remember why Idrees had been there with them that day. But he had been the one that day who told Layla to flee.

Idrees had been the one who separated them.

And now, when Jaffar and Jasmin began preparing for the Archery Battle, who had warned them that the Jannah Jewels were going after the artifacts and the secret of the clock? Who had told them that the Jannah Jewels were dark forces not to be trusted?

Idrees had been the one!

80

But what was it that Jaffar had said? Layla had sent the Jannah Jewels in response to Jasmin and Jaffar, meaning that, in fact, his own children were the dark forces searching for the artifacts. Idrees had turned Khan's children against their own mother!

Khan began to weep and shake. His own brother! After all these years, he could not deny the truth any longer. Idrees had betrayed him.

*　*　*　*　*

Khan rose from his bed at the first rays of dawn, unable to sleep. He made wudhu, prayed Fajr, dressed himself, and walked to Jaffar's bedroom. He knocked on his door.

"As salaamu alaikum, my son, we need to talk, are you there?" Khan said through the door, waiting. "I think you may be right. I think we need to have a serious discussion about your uncle."

Khan waited for Jaffar to open his door, but heard nothing. He knocked a second time, and waited. Then he reached to the knob, and found the door unlocked. When he went in the room, he found the bed had not been slept in, and Jaffar's backpack was gone. There was a note on his bead. Khan picked it up.

Bismillah ir Rahman ir Raheem

As salaamu alaikum my dearest Father,

Uncle Idrees sent Moe and Slim to thwart my mother and my sister. This is a fact I cannot deny, even if you do not believe me. I must believe in what I know in my heart to be painfully true. We both know I must protect my sister. We both know I must protect the secret of the clock, as Mother would want, in sha Allah. My dear Father, please do not be angry with me. I hope you will see the truth as painful as it is. In sha Allah, I will meet you at the Archery Battle. We can save our family together. You can not trust Uncle; though I know it breaks your heart, you know the truth...

Always Your Loving Son, Jaffar

Khan's eyes were filled with tears. His son had grown into such a strong, fearless man. Khan was proud. But he was also worried. Jaffar was still a young man, and this was a very dangerous game Idrees was playing.

"My brother, Khan," a soft voice called behind him. He turned gently, and saw his sister-in-law, Nur, standing in the doorway of Jaffar's room. Their eyes met, and suddenly, she began to sway back and forth as if she was going to collapse.

Khan quickly slid Jaffar's armchair underneath Nur, to catch her. She began to weep openly, sobbing. Her hot, fat tears left trails down her red cheeks. Her body shook with sadness and she struggled to catch her breath. Once she calmed herself, taking deep breaths, she began to explain.

"He's gone, Khan." She said with pain in her voice. "Gone. Last night, he began packing his suitcase. I thought he was just getting ready for the Battle next week. I asked him…"

"I asked him why he seemed upset, and he went hysterical. He was so angry, Khan! Never have I seen him this way! He said that you know! That you and Jaffar both know!"

Nur sounded frightened as she continued. "I asked what he thought you knew. I didn't understand it at all. And then he explained everything. Everything,

Khan, and I couldn't believe it! All these years! He lied to me all these years, to you, to our sweet Layla, to our friends. All these years he betrayed our families. He has been holding this grudge and plotting this for years."

"I was overwhelmed. I began to cry, and grabbed my husband's arm, shaking him. He just looked away. He packed his bag, and told me to forgive him. Then he just walked out." Nur finished, "he walked out with his suitcase, and I didn't know how to stop him. And he's gone, I don't know where."

"It's alright, my sister," Khan handed her a handkerchief to dry her eyes. "It is wrong that your husband has dishonored you this way. You have done nothing but be a great wife, sister, aunt, and friend. Allah will remember your honor and strength."

"My brother Idrees," Khan continued, his voice growing low and deep, "my brother needs to learn that his betrayal has consequences. Already, my son travels to battle his efforts. I too will have to help my son at every turn from this moment forward. Our paths are clear now."

9

Desperate Enemies

For the first time in all of their missions, Moe and Slim truly felt desperate.

"Idrees is going to be so angry," Moe said as he walked at a fast pace.

"So angry," Slim countered. "So, so furious. You heard what they said in the tent. They know the cat is in the bazaar."

"They're going to find that cat."

"I know," Slim sighed.

"You know they are. They're blessed. Their faith is so strong. That cat was special. We are fools."

"And that cat ruined my favorite cloak!" Slim

whined.

Moe stopped in his tracks. He punched Slim on the side of his arm. Slim winced upon contact.

"Are you kidding? You are upset about your cloak? Idrees is going to be furious if these girls get the lamp from the Sultan Mosque. And you're worried about your cloak!"

Slim sat down, looking hurt. "It was my favorite cloak. But you are right. How do we keep fumbling? How is this so hard? Are we really fools?"

"Boss will be very upset," Moe concluded. "We have got to finish this once and for all. Idrees will not accept failure again. So how can we..."

"Oh, no," Slim's voice got tense and nervous, "don't look up now. Wait until you see who just rode a skateboard over that bridge."

"Rats!" Moe screamed. "It's the 14th century, Slim! Egypt in the 14th century! Who else would be riding on a skateboard during this century?"

"Well, then help me catch up to them! It looks like..." Slim yelled as the pair began chasing after the skateboarding girls. "...it looks like 2 of them only. And I don't see a cat. Maybe it's not too late for us."

Moe and Slim chased Jaide and Sara to a crowded river bank crossing. Standing next to the bridge spanning the Nile, the pair of girls were forced to wait while local judges directed traffic over the busy crossing.

"Hey! I know where they are going!" Moe whispered loudly to Slim as they walked through the crowd, trying desperately to get close to the girls.

"Al Azhar is over there, up the hill from the other bank of the Nile. Remember, the girls said they would split up to deliver that key and find the lamp. These two must have the key," Slim concluded.

"Then we've got to get the key before they give it to Ibn Khaldun. Maybe if we get the key, we can trade it for the lamp," Moe guessed.

"Then let us begin," Slim growled, and the pair of bumbling desperate boys made their way to Jaide and Sara, who were standing completely unaware.

Moe swept his cloak in a wide motion and knocked over Jaide. Sara turned to see Slim taking a swing at her with his fist, but she ducked. Jaide rolled over on the ground, confused by the attack. People in the crowd, waiting to cross the bridge, turned, and looked at the commotion.

Sara wriggled away running towards Jaide but before she could reach her, Moe tripped Jaide's feet with a long stick and sent Jaide flying to the floor skinning both her knees. As she made contact with the ground, the silver key fell out of her jacket and flew into the wide open away from her reach.

"I got it! I've got the key, Slim! Let's get outta here before the others show up!" Moe yelled. He wheeled around and began running across the bridge. Slim got up and began racing after Moe.

Jaide pushed herself to her feet, and ran toward the trio, but tripped over a coil of heavy rope at the foot of the bridge. She wiped out on the hard stone and winced in pain. As she looked up, she saw Sara race past Slim. She threw a large rock into Moe's path who stumbled on it knocking the key out of Moe's hand. As Jaide watched, the key slid over the stones and flew off the bridge, falling into the Nile below.

"The key! In the water!" Jaide yelled out. Sara turned, took a giant gulp of air, and lept off the bridge down into the water. Moe and Slim scrambled to their feet and stumbled off, confused and angry. Jaide waited a minute, then two, but Sara did not return to the surface with the key.

"SARA!" Jaide screamed. She reached down to the rope that she had tripped over. She tied the end of it around her ankle, reached down and grabbed a heavy rock, then ran as fast as she could off the edge of the bridge. She splashed into the water, and quickly sank because of the weight of the rock. She sank all the way down to where she could see Sara.

The water of the Nile stung Jaide's open eyes, and she dropped the rock. She swam five feet over to Sara, who was choking without any water. Sara wrapped her arms around Jaide, and Jaide reached down to her foot. She grabbed the rope tied around her ankle and began to follow it up, back toward the sky.

Jaide pulled herself up the rope, while Sara

barely hung onto Jaide's waist. Suddenly, Sara's face burst through the surface of the river, as her friend Jaide pulled her to shore and out of the Nile. Sara was not moving.

Jaide was pale and frightened. She could not tell if Sara was breathing. Jaide pushed on Sara's chest, and shook her friend. She prayed, "Allah, please! No! We have so much more to do to serve You. We have families to love! Please, God!"

Suddenly, Sara coughed loudly, and spit water out of her mouth as she sat up. Jaide helped her friend sit, and patted Sara's back as Sara cleared her lungs and gathered her breath. Soon, the color returned to her face, and Jaide knew her friend would be alright.

"Jaide," Sara gasped between coughs, "I failed. I could not reach the key. It fell so deep, and by the time I got to the bottom where it was sitting, my breath was gone, and I began to shake. I couldn't reach…"

"Shhhhh, my friend," Jaide hugged Sara, rocking her gently while they both dripped wet. "You did the best you could. You are more important than the key. We will have to figure something else out."

"Maybe Hidayah will know what to do," Sara whispered. But she was unsure.

Jaide looked down at the waters of the Nile. The key was surely gone now. And she did not know what Hidayah could do to solve this problem. Even Jasmin would have no trick to fix this.

For the first time in all of their missions, Jaide and Sara truly felt worried.

10

The Glass Lamp

It was a good thing that Muezza knew his way through the Cairo bazaar to get to the Mosque of Sultan Hassan, because without him, the girls would have gotten lost again. They followed the little cat, who occasionally stopped and licked his paws while waiting on the girls to catch up.

The trio of girls reached an open square, and Muezza ran to a set of stairs in front of a massive building. He reached the top step and sat down under a warm beam of sunlight, tucking his paws under his belly. He closed his eyes - a perfect time for a cat nap!

"Is this the Mosque of Sultan Hassan?" Hidayah

asked.

Iman opened her Book of Knowledge and looked up the Sultan Hassan Mosque. Next to the entry, she found a picture of the monumental entrance gate of heavy brick. The doorway was capped by strange carvings shaped like honeycombs.

"This is it!" Iman confirmed. "The Sultan Hassan Mosque is one of the largest in the entire world. It has an open courtyard plan with four attached rooms that served as classrooms and lecture halls, where scholars of all four schools of Islamic law could come and teach students. It is also famous for its stunning hanging lamps in the main prayer hall."

"Those must be the lamps the Commander was describing. Let's go in and catch up on some prayers we have missed while in the desert," Jasmin suggested. "Then we can find someone in the mosque to help us."

The girls entered the first courtyard and performed their ablutions at the beautifully tiled fountain. Then they entered the massive prayer hall and found a quiet area where the women pray.

After completing their prayers, the girls walked to the side of the main prayer room, where the imam was tidying up some of the rugs on the floor. The girls approached the imam.

"Greetings, wise imam. We wanted to thank you for letting us pray in your mosque. We travelled from very far to visit the Mosque of Sultan Hassan," Hidayah explained.

"Where do you come from?" the imam asked.

The girls paused and looked at each other. Jasmin jumped in. "We come from Fes, in the West. I grew up on the hillside of the city itself, near the great Quaraouiyine Mosque."

The imam nodded his head in agreement. "I have heard many good things about Quaraouiyine. Some say it's school is as good as Al Azhar here in Cairo."

"The world is better to have many great homes of learning," the imam continued, "where people can come together and share knowledge and teachings. It's not a competition."

"Our own school is very good as well here at

the Mosque Sultan Hassan. But Al Azhar, over there they have the great scholar Ibn Khaldun lecturing. Hard to compete with that. But we have this beautiful mosque, and that allows us to serve the community."

Iman thought about how much she loved Cairo. It seemed that everywhere she went, there were schools or lectures, many beautiful opportunities to learn. She liked listening to the map lecture in the Mamluk camp. Here in the school attached to the mosque, she could hear students reciting Qur'anic passages. And Al Azhar hosted some of the greatest Islamic minds of all time. Iman knew that Allah's message of knowledge was her core mission in life - to share knowledge with others, and to always be learning.

"Well, we couldn't help but notice that your mosque is very lovely. The fountain for ablutions outside was so ornate and graceful. And we love all these hanging lights," Jasmin complimented the stunning work of architecture. "The hanging lights flicker magically, especially with the color painted on the glass."

"Yes. These enamelled glass lamps are great works of art from our craftsmen. It takes expertise to enamel glass lamps like this. So delicate. I'm so glad you like them," the imam beamed with pride.

"Wait," Iman said. "That's a lamp?"

The imam laughed. "Why of course it is! What did you think a lamp was?" He motioned over to a young mosque worker to come help, then whispered in his ear to get a ladder to bring down a lamp.

The trio of girls all looked at each other nervously.

"Well, I guess I thought of a lamp like in Aladdin, made of metal. A small, metal genie's lamp," Jasmin said, slowly. Hidayah and Iman nodded their heads in agreement.

The imam shook his head in confusion. "Aladdin? Is this one of Scheherazade's tales from Baghdad, the learned city of the East?"

Hidayah's eyes widened, and the other girls fell silent. "Ummmm, yes. Indeed. From Baghdad. We heard it on one of our travels. Sir, we need an enamelled lamp. But one made of metal, not glass. I think the glass will break."

The imam shook his head. "No, my friend, I am sorry, you are confused. You did not ask for an oil wick lamp. Those are made of metal. You asked for an enamelled lamp, no?"

Hidayah pulled out her map and checked the entry for Egypt. Sure enough, it stated "ENAMELLED MAMLUK LAMP". She rolled up the map and nodded.

"Well, enamelled lamps are made of glass. I can get you what you want," the young mosque worker said proudly. The imam nodded his head, and the mosque worker scampered up the ladder to take down one of the hanging lamps.

"So," Iman continued, "these are lamps, enamelled ones like the one we need. What does it mean to be an enamelled lamp?"

The imam smiled. "Our artists, here in Cairo, are the greatest in all the Mamluk lands, who in turn are the greatest in the Muslim world. As you can see on these lamps, thin glass is shaped into the desired form for the lamp. Then, bright colors are painted into patterns and figures, especially ornate calligraphy of Qur'anic verses."

97

"Our painters take gold and silver, and grind them into powders, and mix the powders with the paint. And so when the candles shine through the lamps, the paint sparkles with real metal," the imam continued, his eyes twinkling with excitement.

"But what makes Mamluk enamelled glass so glorious is that other artists must paint each color separately, or the paints melt into each other. Other painters reheat the glass each time which destroys the graceful shape of the glass."

"But our painters created enamels that do not melt together. They use science and knowledge, which is glorious worship of Allah. Our painters use many colored enamels all at once, and only heat the glass once. This is why our enamelled lamps are more colorful and in such strange and wonderful shapes," the imam finished with a smile. "They are lovely enough to illuminate our studies and prayers in true style. We'd love to give you one to remember your time here in Cairo."

"You know who would love this?" Hidayah said sadly. "Jaide would love this. She would love the little details necessary to make such a magnificent piece of art. No one appreciates art with such cleverness as she does."

The girls nodded their heads sadly as they missed their friends. Jasmin prayed that Jaide and Sara were successful in their mission

"And so here is your lamp. I have taken it down for you," the young mosque worker said. He handed Hidayah the lamp, and then took his ladder in his hand. "I've tied the chains above it together so you can carry it hanging in front of you. That is the easiest way to carry it safely."

"So where are you taking it?" the imam asked.

"Uh, Canada?" Iman said reflexively.

"I haven't heard of such a place. Is that West Cairo?" the imam asked Hidayah.

Iman giggled. Jasmin jumped in. "We are taking the lamp to Al Azhar, to talk to Ibn Khaldun. Our friends are with him there now."

"That is good," the imam said, satisfied. "That is not too long a walk. You can get there without breaking this lamp as long as you are careful and avoid crowds. Or camels! My, camels are rough beasts, no?"

"Oh, Allah!" Hidayah took ahold of the chains with both hands, and struggled with the lamp. "This is heavy! You would think it was light, because it's made of glass, but this…" She struggled to get a strong grip on the chains holding up the lamp.

"This is a serious challenge," Hidayah concluded.

Iman felt a soft rub against her ankles and heard a warm purr. She looked down to see their black cat Muezza had returned, ready to lead them on the path to Al Azhar.

"Look who showed up to take us through the bazaar to Al Azhar," Iman joked.

"Though the bazaar… the bizarre…" Jasmin gasped. "The clue! Of course! Through the bizarre market: the bazaar!"

"You're right, Jasmin," Iman exclaimed. "This little fellow will take us right through, just like the clue says!"

"You guys!" Hidayah's voice was excited, loud, and tense. "This lamp is heavy and fragile. Why are we not on our way?"

11

The History of History

Once again, Muezza led the way through the crowded bazaar, but Hidayah struggled to keep up. They avoided the busiest streets, so that no one would bump the lamp. Instead, they walked through the tanners' market, where the leather was sold, and the carpet market, with its open square full of weaving looms.

"Friends, I do not mean to complain, but we are going to have to stop and change who carries this," Hidayah panted. "While we're at it, we should stop for a spot of tea."

The trio stopped at a tea shop just next to the carpet market. They sat around an intricately carved wooden stool upon which stood a shiny metal teapot and clear purple glasses. As they enjoyed the hot, tangy taste of the tea, Iman pulled her Book of Knowledge out of her bag.

"Great idea, Iman," Hidayah chirped between sips of tea. "Let's use our time wisely and learn about where we're going."

"Al Azhar is one of the oldest universities in the world. It was the center of Islamic learning for nearly a millennium, featuring many famous philosophers and theologians. Islamic students and scholars from around the world met there to exchange ideas," Iman read aloud.

"Does your book say anything about Ibn Khaldun?" Jasmin asked.

"Yes. He is known as the "father of history" because of his famous manuscript called *The Muqaddimah*. It was the first book that said that history repeats itself, and that we can learn lessons from the past." Iman continued, "and he said that we must understand historical events within the context of the times they happened in."

"Sounds to me like his wisdom could help guide us on this journey… and perhaps he is the man who unlocks and illuminates men's minds from the clue. Let's go find him at Al Azhar," Hidayah said with excitement.

"Also, ladies, we must remember one more thing," Iman said, with a serious tone of voice.

"Yes?" Jasmin asked nervously. "What other secret could the book hold?"

"We can't tell Jaide that we stopped for tea and cookies. If she finds out we stopped…" Iman's voice faded off and she burst into laughter. Hidayah and Jasmin also began to laugh. All three missed their friends Jaide and Sara, but they knew that the mission required cooperation. But, for so much of the past few days, the girls had to be serious, and it felt good to laugh and smile.

"Oh, you are right," Hidayah said as she wiped a tear from her eye. "Jaide will be positively angry if we don't bring her a bag of cookies too! Let's order some to take with us, and get ourselves on our way to Al Azhar."

"I'll carry the cookies!" Jasmin chimed in. "You're just so good at carrying that lamp, Hidayah! And Iman has to keep following our kitty friend."

"Oh, I knew I'd get stuck with the lamp again. Don't you worry," Hidayah laughed again. "You better carry an awful lot of cookies. Jaide's going to want a lot of cookies when she sees this lamp."

The girls continued to follow their feline friend, bobbing and weaving through crowds until they reached a large, low, white marble building with an onion-shaped dome and fancy minarets. Jasmin caught the attention of one of the young men coming out of the building's main doorway.

"Is this Al Azhar?" she asked.

The young man nodded, "yes, it is. Are you new students?"

"Ummmm, yes. We just arrived from Fes. We were hoping to see Professor Ibn Khaldun. Do you know which classroom he is in?" Jasmin asked slyly.

"Why, of course! He is lecturing in the main hall on in the east wing, past the giant open courtyard. He is lecturing right now - if you run, you may be

able to catch some of his talk!"

"Thank you! We will try," Iman smiled and waved as the girls walked on past and entered the building. They quickly skirted through the main courtyard, looking for the classroom.

"Did you see Sara or Jaide?" Hidayah whispered to her companions. "I didn't see them anywhere."

"Nope," Jasmin whispered back. "But perhaps they are with Ibn Khaldun in the lecture hall. Let's just get there and listen and find our friends after."

Muezza meowed loudly and began to scamper off to a doorway off to the right of the walkway. The girls quickly followed and ducked into the classroom. The room was full, with rows of students sitting on low benches, writing on parchment resting on lap desks. At the front of the room, a middle-aged man with a serious moustache sat on a heavy pillow atop a large stone.

The girls sat down in the farthest back row. Muezza rested under Iman's legs. They listened to Ibn Khaldun speak, and Jasmin smiled. He has a Moroccan accent, she thought.

"You see, it is because history repeats itself that we can see patterns emerge. Dynasties are only good for four generations. The first is the hero king, his son the noble prince. The grandson grows greedy and weak because he lives off his family's luxury, and the fourth generation is corrupt and wasted. Then a new leader must appear," Ibn Khaldun explained.

Jasmin was again reminded of the lesson she learned in the Mamluk camp - that leadership cannot be passed from parent to child, because that does not require the child to be a good leader. It was better to *earn* a position of leadership by being talented.

"Now you ask, how does the hero king win the love of his people? Winning wars, stealing gold? No!" Ibn Khaldun shook his fist in the air. "No! He creates a feeling of *asabiyya*. What's this, you ask? *Asabiyya* is the feeling men feel when they belong to a group, and are proud, and they want to follow a leader because that leader represents them."

"Look at our great Prophet Muhammad, peace and blessings be upon him! His community at Medina followed him because he made them feel *asabiyya*, and showed them that they could be a community that worshipped Allah together, proudly. This is what a good leader does: he creates the bonds of *asabiyya* among all his people," Ibn Khaldun concluded.

Many of the students scribbled notes furiously and nodded in agreement. Ibn Khaldun breathed out, as if the lecture was complete. Hidayah leaned over to Iman and Jasmin.

"Sensei Elle, she is a truly great leader. Think about how she works with the other Masters," she whispered. "They follow her, but there is an easiness about it. Everyone feels like part of the team, like one bonded body, and Sensei Elle is the head."

Iman nodded confidently, "Sensei Elle creates asabiyya. Ibn Khaldun has described her so well."

"You know…" Jasmin's voice trailed off, and was tinged with sadness. "I never saw Mother as a leader. She was just my mother, and my teacher. But she was never my Sensei. I haven't worked with her on missions as you have. So I never got to know what a good leader my mother is. Perhaps I will get the chance to in the future."

"Thank you for sharing these thoughts with me," Jasmin concluded. "I am learning more about my own mother from you. I really am grateful. Allah has blessed me with wisdom and reflection on so many aspects of my life on this mission. It is like I am uncovering the riddle of my own life."

Iman felt tears running down her face. "Jasmin, I am sorry we ever doubted you."

Hidayah shook her head in agreement. "We have so much to learn from you as well. This has been a good experience for all of us. We are glad to have you as one of the Jannah Jewels now. You have made us all stronger in our own faith in each other, and in Sensei, and in Allah's plan for all of us in this."

Hidayah's words moved Iman and Jasmin deeply. They could tell that Hidayah had a natural ability to make everyone feel special and important to the mission. Just as Ibn Khaldun had said, a good leader needed to foster *asabiyya* among the group. Hidayah had that special power, which would help her become a good Master Archer, if only she could win the Archery Battle.

The trio began walking across the room to present the lamp to Ibn Khaldun when a pair of figures burst into the classroom of Al Azhar. Jasmin turned, hand already reaching for her bow, when she smiled.

Finally, Jaide and Sara had arrived, soaking wet.

12

Reunited

Sara and Jaide raced up to the trio of girls, out of breath. They struggled to speak.

"Ladies! So good to see you again! We went to the mosque," Hidayah confirmed. "We got our enamelled lamp. Oh, Jaide, you would have loved to hear about how this lamp was made. We'll tell you sometime, it's fascinating. Hey… why are you both wet?"

Before Jaide could begin to speak, Jasmin interrupted. "Everyone, no time to catch up! Ibn Khaldun is getting up to leave. We must go speak to him." The girls ran over to the great scholar, who was packing some pieces of chalk in a small bag tied to his belt.

"Ibn Khaldun, we greatly enjoyed listening to your lecture on asabiyya and history. It was very enlightening," Jasmin said honestly. "We wish to ask your advice on a problem we have. We were hoping you could illuminate our minds and help us find a solution."

Ibn Khaldun nodded his head and turned his full attention to the set of young women. "I'd be happy to help if I can. What topic may I give you advice on?"

"Well, sir, it's about this lamp," Hidayah began.

"That's a great lamp," Ibn Khaldun noted.

"Yes, sir, it is. It's a great lamp. But, really, that's not what we are confused about. Our problem is, well, that we are travelling great distances through time and space," Jasmin began. Sara elbowed her in the side.

"Travelling great distances, I mean," Jasmin continued. "And we do not know how we can carry this lamp all those great distances. Do you have any thoughts on this problem of ours?"

Ibn Khaldun looked at them sternly, "you cannot expect to carry that with you around the city, let alone around the world. It's a lamp made of glass. It's going to break."

"Yes, indeed," replied Hidayah knowingly. "I've been carrying it for the last two hours. I'm very exhausted, Ibn Khaldun sir. It's fragile and awkwardly shaped. I know we can't keep carrying it around. We hoped you would have some advice on what we should do."

"Yes, I do. Actually, blessed are you, God is surely pleased with you. I happen to have a beautiful metalwork case I bought at the bazaar a few days ago." Ibn Khaldun. "I could give it to you, and pack your lamp inside. That way, you protect the lamp and it becomes easier to carry… wherever you are going to take it."

"Oh, praise Allah! That sounds outstanding," Jasmin cheered. "That sounds like a solution to our problems! And we would love to see this metalwork case you bought, especially if it's Mamluk." The tone in Jasmin's voice suggested to the Jannah Jewels that she was hinting at something.

It suddenly occurred to Iman. What if Ibn Khaldun's trunk was the twelfth artifact? Maybe they did not even have to go to Uzbekistan to get the last artifact for the Golden Clock, and they needed to hurry. Could they get two artifacts at once?

Ibn Khaldun turned around and left the room hurriedly. They girls heard him shuffle his way up stairs down the hall and move quickly. Sara was still struggling to capture her breath; after all, it had only been an hour since she almost drowned in the Nile!

Jaide called out, "Hidayah, Iman, Jasmin, please listen to me and Sara. We must tell you about our mission!"

"Yes, how long have you been here?" Iman interrupted.

"Did you hear Ibn Khaldun's lecture? Did you listen? I found it so informative," Jasmin mused.

Hidayah also joined in, "the way that Ibn Khaldun talked about power, and how good leaders maintain the trust of their people was very interesting."

"No, please, please let us speak!" Jaide begged. Sara tried to join in but had a coughing fit.

Ibn Khaldun came jogging into the room, carrying a shining silver and gold case in his arms. He placed it on a table in front of the girls. He motioned to Hidayah, who brought the lamp over and placed it into the metalwork trunk. Ibn Khaldun removed his cloak and packed it into the case, padding the sides of the glass lamp so that they did not bump against the inside of the case. The lamp was a perfect fit.

"Would you look at that? A solution indeed! With this lamp all packed in, it will stay protected while you travel," Ibn Khaldun exclaimed. Then he reached over and pushed the top of the trunk shut. It clicked satisfyingly.

"This is wonderful. It really is," Sara finally caught her breath. "But I want to talk about our mission."

Jaide wasn't listening to Sara, however. Neither was Jasmin, nor any of the Jewels. They were all distracted examining the ornate, stunning metalwork trunk.

"This trunk is made out of gold and silver, each interwoven to produce a stunning contrast. The metal is worked by hand, in some places hammered and others etched, to create interlocking lines that look like shapes," Ibn Khaldun said. "What makes this piece so amazing are the silver fittings on the two sides that make the handles look like lions. It's such a unique piece. I was going to send it to my friend General Timur in Uzbekistan soon. I suppose I'll find something else for him."

The girls stared at the endless detail on the chest's exterior. Jaide pulled out her sketchpad. She was completely entranced by the metalwork trunk, becoming lost in the curves of the complex patterns and delicately etched flowers. Her pen raced to capture all the little details, ensuring that the calligraphy inscriptions praising the Sultan were copied perfectly.

"While Jaide finishes her sketch, I want to take care of every detail. We appreciate you giving us this case to protect our lamp," Hidayah thanked Ibn Khaldun. "But we obviously will need the key to open it."

"Of course," Ibn Khaldun agreed. "You'll have to talk to Commander Abdullah. He's the one who sold me the case. He had the key over in his tent. He told me a few days ago that, at the first opportunity he had to find a messenger, he would send the key over. But I haven't received it yet."

"Oh, fantastic!" Jasmin exclaimed. "The Commander gave us that key this morning. Jaide and Sara were bringing you that key while we were picking up the lamp, and… wait. Jaide, Sara, why haven't you delivered the key yet? What did you wait for?"

Jaide looked up from her sketch, then froze. "The Commander's key? We can't open the trunk to take out the lamp without the Commander's key?" She looked at Sara, whose face was draining of all color. The pair stood in shock.

"Yes, Jaide," Hidayah affirmed. "Where's the Commander's key?"

Don't miss the next Jannah Jewels book!

Will the Jannah Jewels be able to retrieve the key? How are they going to open up the trunk? Is the trunk truly the 12th artifact that will open up the Golden Clock? Will all 12 artifacts fit inside the Golden Clock? What is the secret? Who will win the famous Archery Battle? What will happen between Khan and Idrees?

Find out the secret of the golden clock and read the exciting conclusion of the Jannah Jewels Book Series - "United in Uzbekistan!"

Find out more about the twelfth book by visiting our website at
www.JannahJewels.com

Glossary

Al Azhar: oldest degree-granting university in Cairo, Egypt

Alhamdullilah: Arabic for 'All praise is for God'

Allah: Arabic for 'God'

Ameen: same as 'Amen,' it is the Arabic word to close a supplication

Asabiyya: refers to social solidarity with an emphasis on unity, and a sense of shared purpose

Bismillah: Arabic for 'in the name of God'

Du'a: Arabic for 'supplication'

Enamelled: to inlay or overlay with enamel (a glassy surface applied by fusion to the surface of metal)

Ibn Khaldun: North African Arab Historiographer and Historian

In sha Allah: Arabic for 'God-willing'

Penultimate: next to the last

Pharaoh: Political and Religious leader of the Egyptian people

Qur'an: sacred scripture of Islam

Salaam: a greeting in Arabic meaning 'peace'

Tasbih: a string of beads tied together to help keep count of one's supplications

Uzbekistan: country located in Central Asia

Ya Hadi: a name of God in Arabic meaning 'The Guide'

IMAN

To find out more about our other books,

go to:

www.JannahJewels.com

Made in the USA
Columbia, SC
21 December 2018